Seasons

The Beautiful Transition

Silas Toney

WestBow Press books may be ordered through booksellers or by contacting:

WestBow Press
A Division of Thomas Nelson & Zondervan
1663 Liberty Drive
Bloomington, IN 47403
www.westbowpress.com
844-714-3454

Because of the dynamic nature of the Internet, any web addresses or links contained in this book may have changed since publication and may no longer be valid. The views expressed in this work are solely those of the author and do not necessarily reflect the views of the publisher, and the publisher hereby disclaims any responsibility for them.

Any people depicted in stock imagery provided by Getty Images are models, and such images are being used for illustrative purposes only.
Certain stock imagery © Getty Images.

Interior Image Credit: Silas Toney

NIV:
Scripture quotations taken from The Holy Bible, New International Version® NIV® Copyright © 1973 1978 1984 2011 by Biblica, Inc. TM. Used by permission. All rights reserved worldwide.

ISBN: 978-1-6642-4705-5 (sc)
ISBN: 978-1-6642-4706-2 (e)

Library of Congress Control Number: 2021920897

Print information available on the last page.

WestBow Press rev. date: 11/30/2021

WESTBOW
PRESS®
A DIVISION OF THOMAS NELSON
& ZONDERVAN

Table of Contents

A Time to;

"*To everything there is a season, and a time to every purpose under the heaven: A time to be born, and a time to die; a time to plant, and a time to pluck up that which is planted; A time to kill, and a time to heal; a time to break down, and a time to build up; A time to weep, and a time to laugh; a time to mourn, and a time to dance; A time to cast away stones, and a time to gather stones together; a time to embrace, and a time to refrain from embracing; A time to get, and a time to lose; a time to keep, and a time to cast away; A time to rend, and a time to sew; a time to keep silence, and a time to speak; A time to love, and a time to hate; a time of war, and a time of peace.*" Ecclesiastes 3:1-8

Acknowledgement

To my Heavenly Father, from whom all blessing flow. Thank You for the many gifts you have given, of them none could compare to Your Son, my Lord and Savior and best friend, Jesus Christ, given as ransom for me. Thank you for the gift of creativity and the means to express Your nature. Whether it be through song, dance, written or spoken word, sculpting or painting, thank You for the vehicles through which we share in releasing Your nature into the entire world. You have the words of eternal life. To know You and make You known. No higher calling I know of!

I want to give special thanks to my children; son TJ and a daughter Celeana. So very proud of both you. Both of you with all your nuances and tendencies are beautiful works of art (Masterpiece's) on display for His glory and splendor. The best is yet come for you. We have walked through many seasons together and we know why we are still standing. Because He made a way. Remember He is the God that keeps and keeps and He keeps on keeping us. He is perfecting all things concerning you. Honor Him with your life, first and always. Love yas.

I want to also give special thanks to family and friends for your encouragement.

Specifically to the friends that I felt safe enough with to share this artistic expression with. Thank you Dr. Madeline Bodoh, Shane Hair, Tennille Wilson and Jennifer Thompson for serving as proofreaders, encouragers and offering valuable feedback for much of the content therein. In addition, want thank all my friends for sharing the beautiful seasons of your life with me. Those times offered more hope and encouragement than can be expressed. Love you.

To Matt Tommey and the Created to Thrive Team. Through your Artist Rise Up Masterclass, I realized that I am an artist, right now! Not only when I become more successful. Not when I become well known as an artist but because I was created as an artist. Right now, along the journey, heaven can be brought to earth through my art. Thank you answering the call to raise up an army of artist to the glory of God.

Preface

Seasons, whether the seasons of life or the four seasons that gives the weather character, all have a distinct purpose. Here, I attempt to bring the four seasons to life in a fun way. I hope to remind some and point others to this truth; everything is made beautiful in its time. To recognize the intentionality of God. The seasons are God's idea!

Summer weather is beautiful June through August, however, not so beautiful September through December. Likewise, winter is not appreciated during the months of summer. However, they all are made beautiful in their time. They are unique by design with character and personality all their own. Each containing their own hidden gems as well as those things we are not as fond of.

Spring, the old renewing, flowers blooming releasing their fragrance while invading the landscape with bouquets of color. Trees interrupt the skyline with every shape and shade of green. New life emerges from the frigid cold of winter. As might be expected, we are not fond of the insects that emerge and the pollen that wreaks havoc on a multitude with allergies; I guess every rose has its thorns.

Summer boast of longer days, family vacation, graduations, 4th of July, fireworks, beach bound and so much more, however, the heat of summer can at times be unbearable, and yet during this time the seeds previously planted continue to take root, grow and produce after its own kind. Oh, how the summer heat can cause one to long for the chill of a fall evening gathered around a fire enjoying a bountiful harvest.

Autumn/fall, the welcome relief from heat and those pesty mosquitos. The fall leaves yield to the moment and cover the landscape with the deep rich colors. Fall temperatures are close to perfect, it has open your window kind of weather. Not to mention the food, the sweet and savory goodness abounds. There is stillness uninterrupted by movement in this season, a sense of rest, a time to gather and give thanks. Fall temperatures prepare us for the harsh winter weather. Imagine the shock to body, going immediately from the heat of summer to the bone chilling cold of winter. Really, the only not so good thing about fall is that it too, ends. By the grace of God, fall and spring are the beautiful transitions between the two extremes.

Often times when we refer to winter, specifically the winter of our lives, we think of cold and colorless with not much growth. As did author Charles Dickens in his famous novel "A Tale of Two Cities" where he vividly captures the perils of the French Revolution and states, "It was the spring hope, it was the winter of despair." Make no mistake; winter has a splendor you should know. Snowcapped mountains, a skier's delight, to the glistening ice cycles hanging from ice-glazed trees, to tulips peeking through the snow with greatest of ease. In addition, that familiar chill in the air, beauty everywhere, yes Christmastime, the most wonderful time of the year. All the while, the moisture that comes from snow and ice in its many forms prepare the earth for spring's renewal. Beauty is woven into the tapestry of every season of life, the good and not so good. Let us endeavor to give authority to that beauty.

For everything, there is a season. He has made everything beautiful in its time. He has also set eternity in the hearts of men (Ecclesiastes 3:11).

l' Alsace Magique

Spring on the horizon, and all days of winter not yet fulfilled! Winter proclaims, "This is my time! Shall not all my days come to pass! After all, are there not four seasons? All the while spring with great expectation awaits her triumphant entry. The excitement at which spring anticipates her moment, expressed in the early budding, hints green invade the skyline, blossoms of color dot the landscape, her fragrance like none other, arises! She can barely stand it! Beautiful is this transition. Cold nights that lead to cooler mornings. Mornings met with coats and sweaters, by noon time garments are shed, welcoming the warmth of the bright sun, and the melodies of a song bird, still teased with an east north easterly breeze just strong enough to fully enjoy the warmness that spring offers and the fading glory of a proud winter. Trees sway in an almost slow motion, liken to a dance in rhythm with the wind, the sun brilliant and soft, evokes smiles of gratitude! Nostalgia overtakes the senses! Cotton candy clouds painted against a magnificently blue canvas, a surprisingly yet inviting kiss on the cheek by the last days of winter and the first days of spring. Spring calls out to winter, no she beckons him "Come away with me, rest and be renewed by first fruits." Winter joyfully surrenders!

"Spring Declares"

The smell of fresh cut grass resting on the wings of an early morning breeze.

Warmth of the sun on my back, the dawning of new day and the chill
of the early morning on my face, directs my gaze upward to find trees
now fully dressed in beautiful shapes and shades of green.

An early morning symphony arises from them, winged musicians usher in the
spirit of gratitude and delight fitting for today's offerings, melodies no man could
compose. Flowers fresh and vibrant adorned with morning dew shimmering
like the purest diamonds, they whisper good morning as I pass by.

Pine needles stand proud glistening in the Rembrandt lighting of the early
and soft sun, its rays tinted with a rustic orange hue. And oh, that flawless blue
sky accented with clouds scattered about with childlike play. The fragrance
of spring in full vigor yielding sweet honeysuckle and blackberry!

Spring declares, "The dress rehearsal is over, if you seek me you will find me!

Spring's Recital

Today's beauty has left me spell bound. My only response was to give praise to God, to thank him for his mighty works, to join creation in declaring His Greatness. The essence of spring rolled up into one day, it appears. She(spring) longs for all to magnify the Lord with her, Oh worship the Lord in the beauty of his holiness has become her theme song, yes, to take moment and just remember who He is. This is the day the Lord has made, shall we not rejoice and be glad in it. For you are worth more than many sparrows and if My eyes are on the sparrow, how could you not know that I am watching over you? Feel the cooling wind on your face, see the trees swaying against the backdrop of the pure blue sky, hear their leaves sing for joy and hear the melody of a spring song as it rides the wings of the soft wind. The sun gently warming the day releasing the fragrance of many blooms as they color the landscape, taste the fruits of spring, blackberries and honeysuckle long to fulfill their purpose!!! They were created with you in mind. The overwhelming presence of peace has captured me, I hear a voice as profound as many rushing waters, and yet as inviting as a sunrise, "I will quiet you with my love, for I rejoice with singing over you (Zephaniah 3:17). You are My treasured possession (Exodus 19:5) and I will never stop doing good to you! Jeremiah 32:40

Summer Breeze

Like a 20 year old longing for their 21st birthday, summer longed for 21 June, its official start. Although summer met with spring weeks ago and danced they did. Spring cautioned summer, you must return, you are not of legal age. Spring asked of summer, what winter once asked of spring; Shall not all my days come to pass? Remember there are four seasons. With the expression of a child wanting to stay up pass their bed time summer retreated, but with hope to wait its appointed hour.

The transition of summer's grand opening, and spring's sweet surrender were bittersweet, enriched with encouragement and thankfulness. Spring declared, "I must decrease that you may increase". With what seemed like a constant breeze, a summer breeze, you know the kind that makes you feel fine while blowing through the jasmine in your mind. Now, enters summer with all the supporting actors. The sun's brilliance now felt all the more, the tranquil blue sky, thick clouds of white holding back their joyous tears on this highly anticipated day, swaying trees with their dancing leaves hum alongside the high and low pitches of song birds, the constant kiss on the face by a refreshing summer breeze inspired responses of beauty and relaxation. People walk about smiling smiles once contained, talk of pool parties, beach trips, 4th of July fireworks, late evening walks in the park, or perhaps a late evening drive just the two of you with no particular destination in mind, homemade mango and pineapple Italian ice. Summer in great demand and with its many opportunities to go, to do, to be, to taste, to look and to see, has a lot be proud of but instead is humbled by this reception, for it knows all too well in a couple of months, Fall (Autumn) shall, once more desire to dance.

(I am not far from you)

There is nothing like a surprise visit from a dear friend! You know the ones you long to see, and try desperately to delay their departure! In the middle of a relentless summer I woke up to a Fall like morning with the low sunlight streaming through my window, a familiar freshness in the atmosphere, every blade of grass adorned with diamonds glistening from the light of the soft sun rising from the east at a true pace. Greeted by a most desired chill in the air, a kiss from a season yet to come, reminding us "I am not far from you" fall declares! I have come to dance with summer! To remind him, in his excitement, he has been a bit harsh; to bring a cooling relief to a parched and dry land. A morning of cool and calm air, oh that gentle breeze on the face that refreshes the soul, no man made invention could match its sincerity, perfectly balanced, when a warm clear day meets a cool clear night and until morning, they do dance! Songbirds make known their pleasure found in this moment offering new melodies, raising a hallelujah louder than any unbelief. Trees now restored and leaves revived making a joyful noise. Oh that summer would surrender, let fall have her way. Fall assures all who long for her coming, "When I come, it will be in all the glory of autumn, with colorful coolness and scented savory sights." God intended that they would seek Him and perhaps reach out for Him and find Him, though He is not far from each one of us (Acts 17:27). Fall proclaims, I am not far from you! Summer, soon we will dance again!

Autumn

Awoken to the coolest morning of summer, it came as a surprise visit accompanied with a soft kiss on the cheek, like the dawning of a new day where new mercies await. Air, fresh like after the rain, an autumn rain. My eyes directed to a fence clothed in morning glory. This breeze, this stillness only found in the long awaited season, autumn, yes, there is a wind that blows only in this season. Inspired praises from a grateful heart, liken to the water turned into wine at the presence of its Creator (John 2:8-9), I blushed and became undone.

This is "Autumn Falling"

Autumn is falling. She approaches with every leaf that makes this time honored descent from branch to ground. Like the seeds that fall from the sower's hand in early spring. Its descent ensures that a multitude shall rise again! Even the leaves understand the wisdom of the moment and yield their entire splendor in glorious hues of deep bright, rich colors, pointing to a splendor greater than thyself. Fall feels like an embrace not too soon forgotten and a smile, smiled just for me. Like holding hands longed to be held.

Autumn has fallen, like the descent of night upon the day; she blew in with an easterly wind, in the still of the night the weight of her presence rested on a city long prepared for her. Summer endured for a night but fall came in the morning! Activities still abound, the farmer and the ant steady preparing and yet a stillness, and a sweet rest calls out to us. Like the kiss of life, like women adorned with colorful scarfs, like a welcomed touch, like an appropriate garment for the season, like a smile that speaks volume, a warm embrace, the crackling of fire, the aroma of baked goods interlaced with spices. Like the gathering of family feasting on seasonal offerings and the experiences of the past year, and even more so, like walking with Him in the cool of day. Fall this is your moment, we welcome you here!

As she gently yet impressively invades the landscape, covering it like a quilt of many colors woven together by grandma's hands. I consider the work of Your hands. Multi-colored corn *like a multi-ethnic congregation beautifully intended, Your masterpiece, like a great harvest reflecting beautiful shades of You. The thought of sweet and savory gatherings come to mind, of those long ago and those yet to come, hopefully bringing snow. Instantly the nostalgia accompanied with the aroma of seasonal offerings flood the senses.*

"Awaken O north wind and come, O south wind. Breathe on my garden, and spread the fragrance of its spices (Song 4:16)." Cinnamon, Clove and All Spice immediately come to mind. They ride on the wings of the wind, calling out like wisdom "Come and sup with me." While powdered sugar adorns a fresh baked pumpkin bread; a hen brined with garlic and rosemary; potatoes, carrots, onions and butternut squash are its roasted companions, sweetened with Mediterranean dates, on a foundation of Jasmin rice, garnished with fresh rosemary and wild cranberries; my kitchen laden with a symphony of aroma. Selah. Like the table set before me in the presence of my enemies, my cup runneth over (Psalm 23:5). I just wrote myself hungry!

Now I, like the deer that panteth for streams of water (Psalm 42:1), so does my palate longs for the first taste of autumn, to be shared with family and friends. As cooler temperatures and a slower pace arrive and plans to gather are made, let us pause to thank the farmer and the trucker whose diligence throughout the spring and summer kept our pantries full and stomachs satisfied. To our teachers, to all the caregivers who fight tirelessly everyday providing quality care and education, for the Soldier (Military men & women) standing guard at home and far, far away. For our clergymen who in the midst of civil/political unrest, dared to proclaim the Truth. To the Giver of every perfect gift (James 1:17) and from Who all blessings flow, be praise, glory and honor forever more. Yea, summer has once again endured for the night, but "Autumn Falls" in the morning!

Winter's Splendor

My time draws nigh. How honored am I, that the greatest of gifts given, given and celebrated during my season, on my watch! I am very familiar with the reason. The hope for all men came forth on a cold winter's night away from earth's eyes heaven came to abide. Even the cold of night could not subdue the warmth of Heaven's light. Although, I am bold and cold, there is a splendor you should know. A chill in the air, trimmed with beauty everywhere. Christmastime is here!

The very thought of snow awakens the child, who screams forget weather mild, "Let it snow, let It snow" we proclaim, from one to 92, just the same! Snow angels and snowmen appear, with watchful eyes standing near. Oh, the wonder that it brings and the memories it makes! Who is it that said? Winter is dead! Have you not a snow sled or snowshoes to tread? As let it snow is chanted, I am reminded of the breath I often take for granted; only seen during winter's splendor, oh now I remember! He, from whom all blessings flow, allowed the winter and sent the snow. Come inside! O how children hate to hear, but frozen are your cheeks! Mom, the snow will be gone next week! Have some coco stated with the warmest grin, and like a symphony "then mom can we do it again? Only in the cold and gray of winter is the sincere hope for the warmth and color of spring. Hope arises! From depths of winter's beauty and sometimes despair, the longing for the first bloom of spring is shared. From the top of snowcapped mountains to the valley of iced glazed trees, winter's splendor begins and beckons all to believe! The weight of her glory on grand display, how beautiful were it to fall on Christmas day. Winter is but a season, a moment and it to passes, liken to vain imaginations and we cast it!

HOW?

In Him, we are a new creature, a new thing
Like flowers in the genesis of spring,
When dead things spring forth life, without any strife
Can dead grass say to itself live again?
Nor can any man free himself of sin.

I AM the ram in the thicket for Abraham
Not of any human device, My Son,
The Messiah, the Perfect Sacrifice.
The one who is 3, the blessed, Holy Trinity

Praise Him for who He is!
Praise Him because He lives!

But how can one be 3?
Nothing is impossible with me.
I AM united without confusion,
Divided without separation,
It was I, who established the earth and its foundation,
The same through all generations

He who clothed Himself in light,
Also separated day from night
God who creates by His will, even

The raging seas remember and are stilled

To the One who has thoughts for me outnumber the sand,
All my tomorrows held in His hands.
His mercy endureth forever!
His love endeth never!

But how? He's God, that's how! He's God, that's how!

Oh death where is your sting?
Our Lord, our Savior, our Risen King,
Defeated hell, death and the grave,
The only name by whom any shall be saved!

JESUS, JESUS, JESUS!

The only begotten Son,
Searched for equal and found none!
For he said of Himself, who is liken to me?
The Father, the Son, the Spirit
Perfect in unity!

Praise Him, Praise Him, And Praise Him!

On bended knee, the only one who can set the captives free!

For it is not by power, nor by might
But by His spirit, every wrong will be made right!
So be not dismayed, for in the midst of two or 3
I am there; I am there, so worship Me!

References

2 Cor 5:17
Genesis 22:13
1 Peter 1:19
Matthew 28:19
John 15:26
Mark 10:27
Psalm 104:5
Psalm 55:19
Psalm 104:2
Hebrew 1:10
Mark 4:39
Psalm 139: 17-18
Psalm 106:1
1 Cor 15:55
Ephesians 1:21
Isaiah 44:7
Isaiah 61:1
Zechariah 4:6
Matthew 18:20
Psalm 89: 9-10

The Seed

Eccl 11:1 tells us to *"Cast your bread on the surface of the waters, [be diligently active, make thoughtful decisions], for you will find it after many days."*

Seeds have different germination periods. Some come up seemingly overnight and others it takes several weeks before you see the breaking of the ground. Likewise in life, we may feel left behind when we fail to see growth, spiritually or otherwise. What we have to remember is, like the physical seed we place in the earth, there is a time component, I know we/I would rather do away with or at least reduce, but time is a crucial component for complete development. Not all seeds, even seeds of the same kind respond to soil in unison. Some will sprout sooner than others. Because we don't see any growth above the soil, we often think that no growth is happening at all, which may cause us to lose heart. We forget that before the stem emerges out and up, roots have to grow down and deep, which supports the weight of everything above the ground. Strong healthy root systems are vital to every plant, not only do they absorb nutrients and moisture from the soil, but also serve as an anchor against the winds that are sure to come. Not to be out done by mere plants, allow Hebrews 16:9 to remind us that *"We have this hope as an anchor for the soul, firm and secure, where Jesus our forerunner has entered on our behalf."* This is one of the reasons why comparing ourselves/our progress to others is utterly useless, we too have different germination periods. When the word of God (the Seed) is planted in the soil of our hearts, for some it may take many days to take root, or accurately apply (fully understand) it in the natural. However, the scripture above assures us that if we are intentional about our growth, we will find it, God will be glorified and others will benefit from our due diligence.

"For just as rain and snow fall from heaven and do not return without watering the earth, making it bud and sprout, and providing seed to sow and food to eat, so My word that proceeds from My mouth will not return to Me empty, but it will accomplish what I please, and it will prosper where I send it. You will indeed go out with joy and be led forth in peace; the mountains and hills will burst into song before you, and all the trees of the field will clap their hands." Isaiah 55:10-12

On 5 Feb 2019, during the State of the Union Address, President Trump spoke in defense of the unborn. This spoke volumes to me, that a sitting president would do such an unpopular thing, and actually calling the recent rulings in New York wrong and stating in front of the world that the unborn are created in the Image of God and deserves to be treated with dignity and respect. They truly are innocent and have no voice lest we give them ours. A couple of days later new numerous bills were introduced and sponsored in the NC Senate and House. The Bills offered the unborn greater protection. I remember praising and thanking God that evening for these victories! I asked Him, something I have never thought to ask before, "What would the unborn say to us could they speak, what would their plea be, to whom would they direct the plea for mercy and their right to live?" Therefore, I began to write.

I am

The Plea of the unborn

I am one who was well known before any of my members were formed.
How Ironic, those who don't know seek to dismember what
was formed to make the known unknown.
However, my image He has engraved in the palms of His hands, He will not forget me.
My walls are forever before Him.
I am one who is remembered, not forgotten.
I am fearfully and wonderfully made, oh that I might live so my soul can know it full well.
I hear of a Royal Priesthood, a Holy Nation, those set apart for the Master's use.
Could He be speaking of me?
Please hear my plea!
Who will stand for me?
Is it not same as standing for Thee?
When you have done it unto the least of these.
You have done so unto me.
Let me live, that His Spirit may dwell in me!
How could my birth be met with such strife?
Are they unaware, I was created by The Way, The Truth and The Life.
His Image on me, now full of worth
This He granted before my birth
Mom, Dad, Church! I am His offspring!
Not some unknown thing.
This you must know! Your own poets have said so!
Knitted together in you, not by man, but with His skillful hands.

Mom you have been lied to this is not the way.
Call on Him I pray, for He is known for making a way out no way.
Oh, church my Savior I long to know, I fear
without your help I will cease to grow.
Will you fight for me?
That I too may proclaim the awesomeness of His name.
I am.

In Christ Alone

From deliverance of the fowler's snare
To becoming heirs and joint heirs
And from the deadly plague,
By who's hands but the Ancient of days?
Covered with His feathers; under His wings
Have now become the most important things
Not even the terror of night nor arrow by day
Shall move me from His holy way!
Like Him, only do what He does and say what He says
From our toiling, turning and striving to have, do and be the best
Jesus beckons all to come to him. "I will give you rest"
An enemy has come in without a trace, fear not
For we have made the Lord our dwelling, our hiding place
He neither slumbers nor is He sleeping, but present, faithful to
Keep, and keep and He keeps on keeping!
So, therefore now there is no condemnation, and no shame
For those who love Me and acknowledge My name
So when the seas of uncertainty rages, even they remember
God's will when we speak it, halt! Be quieted! And peace be still!
Nothing can pluck me from his Hand
Here and now in the power of Christ, I stand
His ministering angels will lift you up, not one foot against a stone
These promises, my children, are found in Christ and Christ alone!

When God wants to Drill a Man

When God wants to drill a man,
And thrill a man, and skill a man
When God wants to mold a man
To play the noblest part;

When He yearns with all His heart
To create so great and bold a man
That all the world shall be amazed,
Watch His methods, watch His ways!

-Anonymous

An Appropriate Time

ECC 3:1 There is a season (a time appointed) for everything and a time for every delight and event or purpose under heaven—

I was just thinking about the question that's often pondered by Christians and perhaps non-believers alike; why did God put the Tree of the Knowledge of Good and Evil in middle of Garden of Eden? He created us knowing temptation would come and yes even sometimes win! We know God is a good God and Father at all times. His timing and our timing are certainly not the same, for His ways are so much higher than our ways (Isaiah 55:9). This is not to irritate us, but to grow us. So, then this question rose up in me, what muscles was God wanting to develop in Adam & Eve? What did they need to exercise so it would become stronger? After all, they knew nothing of the temptation looming just around the corner, neither do we!

What if our wait, our "not now and no" answers to prayer is to exercise and strengthen our spiritual muscles? I believe some of the muscles God wanted to develop were, obedience, complete trust in the spoken word of God, holding it in the highest regard and believing no good thing will He indefinitely withhold from those who walk uprightly. Have you considered that God still wants to build those same muscles in you? When uncertainty, adversity, and the pull of various temptations mount their attack, it's very possible the muscle of faith which causes us to fight the good fight of faith may need to be exercised. For it is with faith we fight, and it is impossible to please God without faith. There is an appropriate time for every good thing we desire (things that are permissible in heaven, therefore permissible on earth). "In Your presence there is fullness of joy; at your right hand pleasures forevermore." God is not a party pooper and Jesus really is the Life of the party!

1 Peter 5:6 Admonishes us to "Humble yourselves, therefore, under God's mighty hand, so in due time He may exalt you."

Galatians 4:4 But when [in God's plan] the proper time had fully come, God sent His Son, born of a woman, born under the [regulations of the] Law), and Romans 5:6 (While we were still helpless [powerless to provide for our salvation], at the right time Christ died [as a substitute] for the ungodly.)

So we can see clearly from the scripture above how important "The appropriate time" becomes for all we are called to do. At the proper time God sent Jesus who was born of a woman and at the "Right time" Christ died for us.

I hope this causes you to remember and smile, I'm sure you can relate. Have you considered the ways in which we are like the One in whose image we are created? Ways in which we unknowingly mimic God. Consider this. Why do we buy our children's favorite food, toy, or whatever, put it in the middle of the home, in full view, and then say to them "Don't touch it until I tell you to, not yet, that's not for right now! Why do we make them wait, what muscles are we wanting to develop in them? Why not let them have everything at the moment of their choosing? That would very quickly become unhealthy for both parent and child. Besides a parents ways should be higher than a child's ways. Could it be the same muscles God wants develop in us during our wait? Patience, which is a beneficial muscle to develop, what about the understanding that there is an appropriate time for everything under the sun. By the way, if this has not been one of the purposes for delaying a good thing, consider making it a part of your purpose, to build muscle memory. God makes it clear that our waiting is not in vain, so we need to do likewise when asking our children to wait. We too are not intending to withhold indefinitely that which is good from our children, but there is an appropriate time to enjoy that favorite thing to the fullest without shame or regret, and with permission from the one who gave it. There is no lasting fulfillment in sneaking it, then feeling guilty, hiding and possibly lying about it. Any satisfaction Adam & Eve experienced from the fruit was short lived, because it was not the appropriate time! Sin is pleasurable, only for a season and then comes death. Fellowship was broken horizontally and vertically. They hid and pointed the finger at each other and even blamed God.

Traditionally, dessert is the last dish served during a full course meal. Have you ever wondered why? In most cases the dessert is proportionately smaller than the appetizer and entre. One more thing about the dessert other than the desire to devour it, it is normally less healthy than the other parts of the meal. It is purposely delayed, not indefinitely withheld, not out of spite, but to maximize the enjoyment of it. It is not wise to fill our bodies with food that's less healthy and leave no room for that which does the body the greatest good. The right foods are extremely important in building and developing strong muscles. There is an appropriate time for dessert.

There is an appropriate time for the beauty of sex to be enjoyed (In the union of marriage between one man and one woman), again this good thing is not intended to be withheld forever, but the creator of this gift intends it for His purpose and our maximum pleasure. Like the dessert, when we consume sex outside of its appropriate time, out of order, it can become unhealthy physically and spiritually as well. Again like the dessert, it will leave no room for that which does the Spirit, body and soul the most good. For when we wait for the appropriate time, God, the giver of every good and perfect gift is glorified, and we reap the greatest benefit and our beds are not defiled. "Marriage should be honored by all and the marriage bed kept undefiled, for God will judge the sexually immoral and adulterers. Hebrews 13:4" Both, the waiting to become one and the consummation of the marriage are worship, beautiful gifts, and this worship is holy and is unto God, there is a most appropriate time for the complete enjoyment of it!

There is an appropriate time for everything.
What muscles does God want to develop in you, in His church during this season?
Remember you were created by Him and for Him.

It's Just a Sentence.

When a season of life is difficult and hard to make sense of, it can really test your patience and question your confidence. Times like these can feel endless. However, this is not all there is. Remember your life is a story and a story consist of words, which creates sentences...etc. Think of time when you had to write an essay or a report maybe in school or on your job, some sentences were more difficult to form than others (Some things are more challenging than others). They were laborious and may have caused you ponder if the effort was worth it or not, but it was just a sentence and with time, you conquered it.

So to you and I believe it's safe to say, also to others, our lives at times can appear to be very similar to that of a undeveloped sentence, one laden with grammatical errors and void of any subject verb agreement, just really hard to understand. In these moments, it is crucial, paramount to remember in whose Hands the pen rest! Our Editor and Chief! We have an Author and Finisher, a Perfecter of faith who is ever interceding for us (Heb 12:2, 7:25). Whispering along the way, "I am with you even to the end of the age."

Even when you feel like you are the run-on sentence, rest assured, at the appointed time and with our cooperation, the Holy Spirit will place the correct punctuation to bring that sentence/season to a close, so you may move on. Remember it was God who begun this good work in you and He is faithful to see it through (Philippians 1:6). Consider Him who endured such hostility from sinners, so that you will not grow weary and lose heart (Hebrews 12:3). Even right now, He is perfecting all things concerning you! Psalm 138:8

Whatever challenge or difficulty you might be experiencing right now or in the future, be encouraged!

It's just a sentence in the story of your life, not your entire book!

Attitude of Gratitude

I am the righteousness of God in Christ Jesus
I am thankful for mobility and dexterity,
For stillness and movement,
For sight and vision,
For sound and hearing,
For a mouth and speaking,
For a heart and loving,
For a mind and thinking,
For breath and breathing
For giving and receiving,
For knowing and being known,
For knowledge and understanding
For eating and tasting,
For life and living,
For death and resurrection
For seeing and beholding,
For health and wealth,
For strength and might,
For Grace and Truth,
For the shaking and the unshakable
For Wisdom and freedom
For space and time
Because I am His and He is mine.

Spring

Sun shining,
Wind blowing,
Birds singing,
Trees swaying,
Grass greening,
Centipede running,
Flowers blooming
Fragrance spreading
Leaves growing,
Sky bluing,
The old renewing.

Autumn

Air chilling
Sun mellowing
Colors deepening
Windows opening
Night's cooling
Harvest abounding
Flavors pleasing
Pumpkin spicing
Leaves falling
Wood burning
Family gathering
Turkey baking
Thanksgiving

God's idea, His Dream

Regardless of the circumstances surrounding your conception, birth or the season of life you maybe in right now, you were God's idea, His dream come true. Before your parents thought to pray and believe for you and even if they didn't and your conception was not a happy surprise. You were always His idea! He was dreaming of you!

Imagine that, God Almighty dreaming of you. You are one of His dreams come true. I knew you even before you were conceived (Jer 1:4–5). Sounds like dreaming to me. I chose you when I planned creation (Eph 1:11–12). You were intended. For all who feel like a mistake, God made it very clear that you are not. You were not a mistake, for all your days are written in My book and ordained for me before one of them came to be (Ps 139:15–16) Our days were ordained for us. The days were created for you, not you for the days. The Sabbath was created for man, not man for the Sabbath (Mark 2:27). For the Son of Man is Lord of the Sabbath (Matthew 12:8) and even when your heart fails you, the Lord declares, "I am greater than your heart".

I determined the exact time of your birth and where you would live (Acts 17:26). You are here and now, for such a time is this. Which includes the biological family you were born into and the spiritual family you belong to, the neighborhood, the school you attend, even the job you have, all are for such a time as this. You are fearfully and wonderfully made (Ps 139:14). His workmanship, a Masterpiece (Eph 2:10). The earth is the Lord's and the fullness thereof (1 Cor 10:26). The world is God's art gallery and we are the priceless original works of art on the display, reflecting His glory and splendor. Beauty in the unity that was derived from diversity. I knit you together in your mother's womb (Ps 139:13), and brought you forth on the day you were born (Ps 71:6). I designed you for My glory, all My good pleasure I will accomplish (Isaiah 46:10). You are as I intended (height, ethnicity, weakness and strengths). My plan for your future has always been filled with hope (Jer 29:11), because I love you with an everlasting love (Jer 31:3). Christ in you is the hope of glory (Col 1:27), that you are filled with. *The richest required to ransom our souls could not be found on earth, so I sent Jesus, heaven's best, a ransom for many. (Jer 31:3). My thoughts toward you are as countless as the sand on the seashore (Ps 139:17-18), be certain that all His thoughts toward you are good and I rejoice over you with singing (Zeph 3:17).I surround you with songs of deliverance. I will never stop doing good to you (Jer 32:40) I the Lord your God changes not (Malachi 3:6), there is no shadow of turning in me (James 1:17), for you are My treasured possession (Ex 19:5). My blood is the receipt and proof of my purchase. Those whom the Father has given Me, no one can snatch them out of My hands. You are Mine! The Father and I are One.*

This is true if you had parents who with great anticipation prayed for your arrival, desired, and longed for you. For those who had a baby shower, bassinet's and a room decorated just for them, equally true for those who may have been an afterthought. True for those that are labeled unwanted. You may have just escaped death on an abortionist table, even those who did not escape, they too were God's idea, His dream, perhaps you were left in a dark alley, or on a doorstep. You may have been told "I never wanted you." You are God's idea, whether born in riches or in extreme poverty, and anywhere in between. Jesus understands you. He the greatest of all kings was born in the humblest of places, with no medical staff on call. In the company of animals He was born. It's possible that the manger baby Jesus rested on was saturated with the saliva of the animals that ate from it.Yet, there the Savior of the world, the ransom for many, laid. These real life circumstances could not rob Him of His identity, nor did it determine or change His destiny. So it is and can be for us. For the abused and misused, those full of confidence and those feeling weary in well doing, to ones who don't understand why the good you desire to do escapes you and yet the bad you don't want to do, seems to cling to you, for the bound and the free. We are not the source of the value placed on us, therefore, we cannot alter the value placed on us! You were my idea, I fashioned you! I called you! You are my dream come true.

And we, who with unveiled faces all reflect the glory of the Lord, are being transformed into His image with intensifying glory, which comes from the Lord, who is the Spirit. (2 Cor 2:18)

Called

"See, I have called by name Bezalel, son of Uri, the son of Hur, of the tribe of Judah. I have filled him with the Spirit of God in wisdom and skill, in understanding and intelligence, in knowledge, and in all kinds of craftsmanship, to make artistic designs for work in gold, in silver, and in bronze, and in the cutting of stones for settings, and in the carving of wood, to work in all kinds of craftsmanship." Exodus 31:2-5

Called – Publicly proclaim
Bezalel - In the shadow and protection of God
Uri - Fiery light
Hur- Purity
Judah – Praise

We were called by name, publicly into the shadow and protection of almighty God as fiery lights. Called into purity producing and giving praise to the God of our Lord and Savior Jesus Christ. Created in His image, now filled with His Spirit in wisdom, in understanding and intelligence, in knowledge and skill for every good work!

I am as dark as the Tents of Kedar as strong as the Cedars of Lebanon. A tree planted by the very hand of God (Numbers 24:6). I reside on the banks of the river that flows with faith, my leaves shall not wither, and whatever I do shall prosper (Psalm 1:3). Lord, You alone are my portion and my cup (Psalm 16:5); You make my lot secure. In You, I live move and have my being, I am Your Offspring (Acts 17:28)!

Silas Toney

Printed in the United States
by Baker & Taylor Publisher Services